Arabic Musical Scales

Basic Maqam Teachings

by Cameron Powers

Audio CD's Not Included
To Order See Back of this Page

To Order the Two Audio CD's:

Use Internet:
Go to: http://www.musicalmissions.com/teachingCDs.html
1) place order with Credit Card for CD's only
2) Include your Shipping Address
3)   If in USA: $19 ($15 plus $4 shipping and handling)
       If outside of USA: $23 ($15 plus $8 shipping and handling)

OR

Send Check or Money Order To:
GL Design
2090 Grape Ave
Boulder, CO 80304

1) Include your Shipping Address
2)   If in USA: $19 ($15 plus $4 shipping and handling)
       If outside of USA: $23 ($15 plus $8 shipping and handling)
3) Include note requesting "Arabic Musical Scale CD's"

OR

Wire Funds To:
Chase Bank, 2500 Arapahoe Ave, Boulder, CO 80302, USA
Account Name: GL Design
Account No: 1025877125
ABA Routing No: 102001017

Note: The Middle Eastern Lute (Oud) is used on the CD's to record all of the scales, modulations and improvisation information covered in this book. Any instrument, including the human voice, may be used to imitate the recorded notes. Instruments capable of playing only well-tempered notes will be able to play 23 of the 45 scales. In order to play the other 22, the instrument must be pitch-adjustable so that "quartertone" pitches (such as E half-flat or F half-sharp) can be produced.
Email for more info: distrib@gldesignpub.com

Arabic Musical Scales: Basic Maqam Teachings, 1st Edition
(Audio CD's not included)

Copyright © 2005 by Cameron Powers
Published by GL Design, Boulder, Colorado. USA

All rights reserved. No part of this book may be reproduced in any form or by any electronic or mechanical means including information storage and retrieval systems without permission in writing from the publisher, except by a reviewer, who may quote brief passages in a review.

Library of Congress Control Number: 2005910058
ISBN: 0-9745882-4-5
ISBN Complete: 978-0-9745882-4-7

Introduction *CD Disk 1 Track 1*

This is an introduction to the world of maqams, or Arabic musical scales. I will be illustrating more than 40 different maqams, and I will be using the oud on the accompanying two cd's to illustrate the pitches of the notes involved.

Do Re Mi Fa Sol La Si Do are the terms used to label notes in the modern Middle East. These come from European "Solfege" and have largely replaced the use of the older Arab note names. Nevertheless, these Arabic note names are provided in a table at the end of this book as advanced students and Arab-world musicians do still know and use them. Arab musicians may know the Western note names C D E F G A B but they are more familiar with the solfege labels.

And, of course, in the world of maqams there are some notes which we refer to as "quartertones." They have degrees of flatness or sharpness which are more or less halfway between the well-tempered notes. The term in the Middle East, again borrowed from Europe, for "flat" is "bemol." The term for "sharp" is "diaz." And the term for "half-flat" is "nuss bemol" or "reboton" or sometimes "sikah." "Nuss diaz" means "half-sharp."

Middle Easterners who've grown up with maqam-based music don't think of particular notes as being "half-flat" or "half-sharp." That's an invention for those of us who are anchored in well-tempered systems. So until we become accustomed to maqams and the intervals that they contain, we run the risk of playing a note which will sound a little bit sour to them. And they won't necessarily know that it's because we are fighting to get away from our well-tempered programming that we are having a problem. The names of the basic notes in Arabic (see Table A) make it clear that for them the E half-flat and B half-flat are more fundamental than the nearby well-tempered notes Eb, E, Bb and B which sound so familiar to Westerners.

In Turkish maqam teachings a system is used which divides whole steps up into 9 intervals called "komas." Degrees of sharpness and flatness can be very finely described that way. I'm going to use the simpler Arabic version of referring to notes as "half-flat" or "half-sharp." Just how flat or sharp notes tend to be played depends on the group of musicians you're playing with. It's possible, I think, to generalize and say that in Turkey the quartertones are played a little bit sharper than in the Arab world, but that's not always the case.

Sometimes in the teachings of maqams, "ascending scales" are shown with sharper pitches than "descending scales." In other words there may be a half-flat or a natural on the way up the scale and a full flat on the way down. There are no hard and fast rules around this. The point is that, in composition or in improvisation, we are free to sharpen or flatten notes in maqams in an ornamental or decorative sense and that is done all the time. I will use a "+" and "-" sign to indicate very tiny changes in pitch.

Of course these maqams are most easily played on fretless instruments like my oud, or like on a violin or a cello... or on open-holed flutes such as they have in the Middle East (the nay or ney). If you're working on a keyboard you may have to program pitch adjustments. And if you're working on keyed wind instruments like clarinet, for example, the bending of the notes can be accomplished by using different key arrangements and by using the strength of the embouchure on the reed. Of course, the human voice is an ultimately flexible instrument. However, if you've grown up in the West, then your natural tendency will be to land on the well-tempered notes and you'll find that it's difficult and that it takes some training to learn to sing notes which fall "in between" well-tempered notes.

The most commonly used quartertone notes are the E half-flat and the B half-flat... and sometimes the A half-flat and the F half-sharp. Frequently in describing a maqam it's only necessary to define intervals of 3 or 4 or 5 notes and so we can talk about "trichords" or "tetrachords" or "pentachords" ("ajnas" in Arabic) and that's frequently done in the language surrounding the teaching of maqams.

Harmony is not given much attention in Arabic composition, although that's changing as more and more influence from the West penetrates. But Arabic music is very much more involved with the intricacy of the melody line and the decorations, the calls and responses, and the pushing and pulling against the rhythmic infrastructure.

Like anywhere else in the world, simpler folk tunes which come from village regions are usually done in one maqam with few changes in the structure of the scales, but the more complex compositions from the larger cities (Like Cairo and Istanbul) and from traditional musical hot-spots (like Aleppo, Syria) include varieties of complex maneuvers from one maqam to another. And it's the job of a Middle Eastern musician, when it's his turn to do an improvisation, or "taqasim," to see if he can artfully show the transitions from one maqam to another and then modulate back to the original maqam. Taqasims usually open with certain trademark riffs (shakhsiyyah) which serve to identify the home-base maqam. Traditional hallmark melodies (dulabs) can also serve this pupose of identifying a maqam at the beginning of a song. From there the musician works (al amal) the transitions and modulations in ways that reflect both a knowledge of tradition and personal innovation until the taqasim is brought to a close back in the home-base maqam with traditional ending phrases (qaflat). The Arab or Turkish audience oohs and aahs at appropriate moments when the traditional and the individual qualities are intermixed.

There are 4 basic groups of maqams. One group is taught with D, or Re, as a tonic, or base beginning note, and another group is taught with C, or Do, as the tonic. There are also groups of maqams based on Bb and on E half-flat.

Each maqam in this book is described by naming the notes with traditional Western names (A through G) and Solfege names (Do through Si). The step intervals between these named notes are also indicated by fractions such as 1/4, 1/2, 3/4, 1, 1 1/4, and 1 1/2.

Of all the maqams described in this workbook, familiarization with the 17 which are in **Bold Print** will suffice to provide a substantial beginning knowledge of Arabic musical scales.

Transposing maqams to different keys yields additional groups of scales based on other tonics and is commonly done to help enable both traditional and artful modulations from one maqam to another. These transpositions frequently involve moving the tonic of one of the 4 basic groups up or down a fourth or a fifth, which is an interval of 4 or 5 notes. Detailed instructions for this come toward the end of this book.

Of course transpositions are also commonly made to match the range of a particular singer's voice. The entire system of maqamat can be moved to any pitch by skilled musicians.

There are maqamat which begin on a D and move up through the next octave and a half without ever including a higher D. This is rare but it does happen and this illustrates the complexity of the tradition. Where maqams go when they get up into higher octaves is sometimes defined but there is enough variety from one teaching to another to make that subject controversial.

Similarly, where maqams go below their tonics and the leading tones below can depend on a variety of structures in an individual song. It is not uncommon for a repetitive bass sequence involving G, A, B half-flat, C, D to underly D-based maqamat which don't even include a B half-flat or other quartertones.

Arabic music is highly decorated with little musical comments and frills, some designed to be obvious while others are played almost subliminally, like "the wink of an eye" (ghammaz). These decorations, combined with the capacity of an Arab singer to sing complex long phrases without ever needing to take a breath, lead into a dazzling array of emotional territories. Many of these emotions are not easily found in Western musical traditions. By listening and living in Arab-speaking countries, these emotional worlds can be brought to life. And whichever musical instrument you play, an endless series of delightful discoveries awaits those who enter the world of Arab maqam music.

Notes:
The Arabic plural of the word "maqam" is "maqamat." By adopting the word into the English language we create the plural word "maqams." Both plural forms are used interchangeably in this book.

Spelling in English, using the Roman alphabet, is only a rough approximation of actual Arabic spelling. You will find names of maqamat and other Arabic musical terms spelled in varieties of ways. There is no "correct" way to spell Arabic terms in English.

This book is an expanded version of "Basic Maqam Teachings" which was first distributed in 2001.

Table of Contents

Note: Familiarization with Maqams named in **Bold** are recommended for **Basic Knowledge**.

D & C & Bb & E half-flat -- Based Maqamat
CD Disk 1 of 2 -- Tracks Listed Below

Track 1:	Introduction	3

D--Based Maqamat

Hijaz Family:

Track 2:	**Hijaz**	9
Track 3:	Hijaz Gharib	9
Track 4:	Hijaz Awji	10
Track 5:	**Shehnaz**	10

Kurd Family:

Track 6:	**Kurd** (Phrygian Mode)	11
Track 7:	Shehnaz Kurdi	12

Bayyati Family:

Track 8:	**Bayyati**	13
Track 9:	**Husayni**	14
Track 10:	Shuri (Turkish Karjigar)	14
Track 11:	**Saba**	15
Track 12:	Saba Zamzamah	15
Track 13:	Saba Busalik	16
Track 14:	Quartertone Practice	16

C--Based Maqamat

Nahawand Family:

Track 15:	**Nahawand** (Natural & Harmonic Minor) (Aeolian Mode) (Turkish Nihavent)	17
Track 16:	Nahawand Kabir (Dorian Mode)	18

Rast Family:

Track 17:	**Rast**	19
Track 18:	Mahur or Kirdan	20
Track 19:	**Suznak**	20
Track 20:	Suzdilar	21
Track 21:	Nerz Rast	21
Track 22:	Rast Beshayer	22
Track 23:	Dalanshin	22

Nawa Athar Family:

Track 24:	**Nawa Athar** (Turkish Nevaser)	23
Track 25:	Athar Kurd	24
Track 26:	**Nakriz** (Zawil, Basandida)	24

Bb--Based Maqamat

Ajam Family:
Track 27: **Ajam Ushayran** (Bb Major) 25
Track 28: Shawq Afza 26

E half-flat--Based Maqamat

Sikah Family:
Track 29: **Huzam** 27
Track 30: **Sikah** 28
Track 31: Mustaar 28

Transpositions & Modulations
CD Disk 2 of 2 -- Tracks Listed Below

Transposed D--Based Maqamat:
Track 1: **Hijaz Kar** (Shehnaz on C) 29
Track 2: Zanjaran (Shehnaz on C with Ajam) 30
Track 3: Shad Araban (Shehnaz on G) 30
Track 4: Suzdil (Shehnaz on A) 31
Track 5: Jaharkah Turki (Shehnaz on F) 31
Track 6: Hijaz Kar Kurd (Kurd on C) 32

Transposed C--Based Maqamat:
Track 7: **Farahfaza** (Nahawand on G) 33
Track 8: Busalik (Nahawand on E) 34
Track 9: Yaka (Rast on G) (Rast Nawa) 34
Track 10: Hisar (Nawa Athar on D) 35

Transposed Bb--Based Maqamat:
Track 11: Jaharkah (Ajam on F) (F major) 36

Transposed E half-flat--Based Maqamat:
Track 12: **Rahat el Arwah** (Huzam on B half-flat) 37
Track 13: Bastanikar (Huzam on B half-flat with Saba) 38
Track 14: Irak (Huzam on B half-flat with Bayati) 38
Track 15: Farahnak (Sikah on B half-flat) 39

Modulations:
Track 16: D -- Based Maqam Modulations 41
Track 17: C -- Based Maqam Modulations 42
Track 18: Transposing and Modulating between D and C -- Based Maqamat 43
Track 19: D Maqams plus Rahat el Arwah 44
Track 20: Sample Modulations 45

Table A: Note names of basic Arabic scale 46
Table B: Note names of expanded basic Arabic scale 47
Pitch Control in Traditional Arab-world Instruments 48
Pitch Control on Other Instruments 50
Glossary 51
Acknowledgments 54
Biography 55

D-Based Maqams
Hijaz Family

Associated Moods:
The Hijazi region of Saudi Arabia is desert. This maqam is associated with the lonely treks of the camel caravans and with fascination and enchantment with the East and its beauty. Very commonly used in popular dance and folk music as well as in religious music and the call to prayer. Has been called simple, pretty, pastoral.

Hijaz   *CD Disk 1 Track 2*

D	Eb	F#	G	A	Bb	C	D
Re	Mi bemol	Fa diaz	Sol	La	Si bemol	Do	Re
1/2		1 1/2	1/2	1	1/2	1	1

Possible Descriptions: Hijaz tetrachord on bottom; nahawand pentachord on 4th; kurd tetrachord on 5th.

Hijaz Gharib   *CD Disk 1 Track 3*

D	Eb+	F#-	G	A	Bb	C	D
Re	Mi bemol	Fa diaz	Sol	La	Si bemol	Do	Re
1/2+		1 1/2-	1/2+	1	1/2	1	1

Possible Descriptions: Hijaz tetrachord on bottom; kurd tetrachord on 5th; nahawand pentachord on 4th.
"Gharib" means "old." So this is the "old" version of hijaz. Before the well-tempered 1 1/2 step interval became common, musicians tended to shrink the interval a little bit by slightly raising the Eb (Eb+) and slightly lowering the F# (F#-). To Arab ears it still sounds better to play the "old" interval.

Hijaz Awji

CD Disk 1 Track 4

D	Eb	F#	G	A	B half-flat	C	D
Re	Mi bemol	Fa diaz	Sol	La	Si nuss bemol	Do	Re
1/2		1 1/2	1/2	1	3/4	3/4	1

Possible Descriptions: Hijaz tetrachord on bottom; rast pentachord on 4th; bayyati tetrachord on 5th.

Many songs are played in this maqam. Musicians may simply state that the song moves from "Hijaz on Re" to "Rast on Sol" at some point during the song without actually knowing the name of this maqam.

Shehnaz

CD Disk 1 Track 5

D	Eb	F#	G	A	Bb	C#	D
Re	Mi bemol	Fa diaz	Sol	La	Si bemol	Do diaz	Re
1/2		1 1/2	1/2	1	1/2	1 1/2	1/2

Possible Descriptions: Hijaz tetrachord on bottom; hijaz tetrachord on 5th; nakriz pentachord on 4th.

D-Based Maqams
Kurd Family

Associated Moods:
The Kurdish people live in present day southern Turkey, Northern Iraq and western Iran. Presumably this maqam is associated with them. Indeed, songs from southern Turkey are frequently in this maqam. The mood varies from gently romantic, sweet and pleasant, to more powerfully exciting and dance oriented, to association with extreme longing in love songs.

Kurd (Phrygian Mode)   CD Disk 1 Track 6

D	Eb	F	G	A	Bb	C	D
Re	Mi bemol	Fa	Sol	La	Si bemol	Do	Re
1/2		1	1	1	1/2	1	1

Possible Descriptions: Kurd tetrachord on bottom; kurd tetrachord on 5th; nahawand pentachord on 4th.

Shehnaz Kurdi

CD Disk 1 Track 7

D	Eb	F	G	A	Bb	C#	D
Re	Mi bemol	Fa	Sol	La	Si bemol	Do diaz	Re

  1/2   1   1   1   1/2   1 1/2   1/2

Possible Descriptions: Kurd tetrachord on bottom; hijaz tetrachord on 5th.

D-Based Maqams
Bayyati Family

Associated Moods:
Romantic, very popular maqam in both Arabic and Turkish worlds. The chanting of the Quran begins and ends in Bayati. Folk singing from southern Turkey, as well as the ashik, or Turkish sufi music, is frequently in this maqam. Common in wedding songs. Husayni, Shuri and Saba are all closely related maqams.

Bayyati   *CD Disk 1 Track 8*

D	E half-flat	F	G	A	Bb	C	D
Re	Mi nuss-bemol	Fa	Sol	La	Si bemol	Do	Re
3/4	3/4	1	1	1/2	1	1	

Possible Descriptions: Bayyati tetrachord on bottom; Kurd tetrachord on 5th; Nahawand pentachord on 4th. The E half-flat in Bayyati is very slightly lower than the E half-flat in Rast and Sikah. When Bayyati is played in higher registers with more emphasis on descending scales, it is sometimes called Mohayar.

Husayni

CD Disk 1 Track 9

D	E half-flat	F	G	A	B half-flat	C	D
Re	Mi nuss-bemol	Fa	Sol	La	Si nuss-bemol	Do	Re
3/4	3/4	1	1	3/4	3/4	1	

Possible Descriptions: Bayyati tetrachord on bottom; bayyati tetrachord on 5th; rast pentachord on 4th.

This maqam is very basic. Like maqam Rast, it includes only original Arab-world notes and intervals.

Shuri

CD Disk 1 Track 10

D	E half-flat	F	G	Ab	B	C	D
Re	Mi nuss-bemol	Fa	Sol	La bemol	Si	Do	Re
3/4	3/4	1	1/2	1 1/2	1/2	1	

Possible Descriptions: Bayyati tetrachord on bottom; Hijaz pentachord on 4th.
Used as an ornament inside of Bayyati. Called Karjigar in Turkish.

Saba

CD Disk 1 Track 11

Associated Moods:
Very powerfully mystical mood. Very different from Western scales. Used extensively in Sufi music. Sad, moving, sincere, tender. Common in folk music.

D	E half-flat	F	Gb	A	Bb	C	Db
Re	Mi nuss-bemol	Fa	Sol bemol	La	Si bemol	Do	Re bemol
3/4	3/4	1/2	1 1/2	1/2	1	1/2	

Possible Descriptions: Bayyati trichord on bottom; Saba tetrachord on bottom; Shehnaz maqam on 3rd. The notes above Db are E, F, Gb. (The E half-flat doesn't necessarily repeat in the high part of the maqam.)
Can be used as an ornamentation inside bayyati.

Saba Zamzamah

CD Disk 1 Track 12

D	Eb	F	Gb	A	Bb	C	Db
Re	Mi bemol	Fa	Sol bemol	La	Si bemol	Do	Re bemol
1/2	1	1/2	1 1/2	1/2	1	1/2	

Possible Descriptions: Kurd trichord on bottom; Shehnaz maqam on 3rd.
This version of Saba can be played on well-tempered instruments.

Saba Busalik

CD Disk 1 Track 13

D	E	F	Gb		A	Bb		C	Db
Re	Mi	Fa	Sol bemol		La	Si bemol		Do	Re bemol
1	1/2	1/2	1 1/2		1/2		1	1/2	

Possible Descriptions: Nahawand trichord on bottom; Shehnaz maqam on 3rd.
This version of Saba can be played on well-tempered instruments. Frequently heard in Greek rebetika music.

Quartertone Practice

CD Disk 1 Track 14

Listen to the CD to practice playing and hearing the differences between Eb, E half-flat and E natural as they occur in the note sequences:

D	Eb	F
D	E half-flat	F
D	E	F

C-Based Maqams
Nahawand Family

Associated Moods: Nahawand is a straightforward and sweet maqam. It is the same as the Natural Minor and the Harmonic Minor in Western music. Common in love songs. Delicate, sweet, tender, sentimental, sad.

Nahawand (Natural & Harmonic Minor) (Aeolian Mode) (Turkish Nihavent)
CD Disk 1 Track 15

C	D	Eb	F	G	Ab	Bb or B	C
Do	Re	Mi bemol	Fa	Sol	La bemol	Si bemol or Si natural	Do
1	1/2	1	1	1/2	1 or 1 1/2	1 or 1/2	

Possible Descriptions: Nahawand tetrachord on bottom; Nahawand pentachord on 4th...
or: Nahawand pentachord on bottom; Hijaz tetrachord on 5th.
Some say that the 3rd note in Nahawand (the Eb) is slightly flatter than in the Western Minor scale.

Nahawand Kabir (Dorian Mode)

CD Disk 1 Track 16

C	D	Eb	F	G	A	Bb	C
Do	Re	Mi bemol	Fa	Sol	La	Si bemol	Do
	1	1/2	1	1	1	1/2	1

Possible Descriptions: Nahawand tetrachord on bottom; Nahawand tetrachord on 5th.

C-Based Maqams
Rast Family

Associated Moods: Common in religious music, call to prayer. Romantic and positive, cheerful, stately and elegant. Classical. Beautiful landscapes, morning or daytime energy. Joy, liveliness, gravity, dignity, enthusiasm, courage, exhaltedness, austere joy, unflinching zeal, strength, vigor, burning passion. Suznak, Suzdilar, Nerz Rast, Rast Beshayer, Dalanshin and Zawil are all commonly employed during brief modulations within Rast.

Rast   CD Disk 1 Track 17

C	D	E half-flat	F	G	A	B half-flat	C
Do	Re	Mi nuss-bemol	Fa	Sol	La	Si nuss-bemol	Do
	1	3/4 3/4	1	1	3/4	3/4	

Possible Descriptions: Rast pentachord on bottom; Rast tetrachord on 5th; Bayyati tetrachord on the 2nd; Husayni maqam on the 2nd; Bayyati trichord on the 6th; Sikah maqam on the 3rd. This maqam is very basic. Like maqam Husayni, it includes only original Arab-world notes and intervals. The E half-flat in Rast is very slightly sharper than the E half-flat in Bayyati.

Mahur (Kirdan)

CD Disk 1 Track 18

C	D	E half-flat	F	G	A	B	C
Do	Re	Mi nuss-bemol	Fa	Sol	La	Si	Do
1	3/4	3/4	1	1	1	1/2	

Possible descriptions: Rast pentachord on bottom; Ajam tetrachord on the 5th.

Suznak

CD Disk 1 Track 19

Associated Moods: Longing, desire, agony, burning, sorrow, grief.

C	D	E half-flat	F	G	Ab	B	C
Do	Re	Mi nuss-bemol	Fa	Sol	La bemol	Si	Do
1	3/4	3/4	1	1/2	1 1/2	1/2	

Possible Descriptions: Rast pentachord on bottom; Hijaz tetrachord on 5th; Huzam maqam on the 3rd. Very frequently used as ornament in Rast.

Suzdilar

CD Disk 1 Track 20

Associated Moods: Soft and tender joy.

C	D	E half-flat	F	G	A	Bb	C
Do	Re	Mi nuss-bemol	Fa	Sol	La	Si bemol	Do
1	3/4	3/4	1	1	1/2	1	

Possible Descriptions: Rast pentachord on bottom; Nahawand tetrachord on 5th. Used as ornament in Rast.

Nerz Rast

CD Disk 1 Track 21

C	D	E half-flat	F	G	A half-flat	Bb	C
Do	Re	Mi nuss-bemol	Fa	Sol	La nuss-bemol	Si bemol	Do
1	3/4	3/4	1	3/4	3/4	1	

Possible Descriptions: Rast pentachord on bottom; Bayyati tetrachord on 5th. Used as ornament in Rast. Also called Nairuz.

Rast Beshayer

CD Disk 1 Track 22

C	D	E half-flat	F	G	Ab	Bb	C
Do	Re	Mi nuss-bemol	Fa	Sol	La bemol	Si bemol	Do
1	3/4	3/4	1	1/2	1	1	

Possible Descriptions: Rast pentachord on bottom; Kurd tetrachord on 5th.
Used as ornament in Rast.

Dalanshin

CD Disk 1 Track 23

C	D	E half-flat	F	G	A	B half-flat	C	Db
Do	Re	Mi nuss-bemol	Fa	Sol	La	Si nuss-bemol	Do	Re bemol
1	3/4	3/4	1	1	3/4	3/4	1/2	

Possible Descriptions: Rast pentachord on bottom; Saba tetrachord on 6th.
Used as ornament in Rast.

C-Based Maqams
Nawa Athar Family

Associated Moods: Enchantment, delicate, amorous affection.

Nawa Athar (Turkish Nevaser)   *CD Disk 1 Track 24*

C	D	Eb	F#	G	Ab	B	C
Do	Re	Mi bemol	Fa diaz	Sol	La bemol	Si	Do
1	1/2	1 1/2	1/2	1/2	1 1/2	1/2	

Possible Descriptions: Nakriz pentachord on bottom; Hijaz tetrachord on 2nd; Hijaz tetrachord on the 5th.

Athar Kurd

CD Disk 1 Track 25

C	Db	Eb	F#	G	Ab	B	C
Do	Re bemol	Mi bemol	Fa diaz	Sol	La bemol	Si	Do
1/2	1		1 1/2	1/2	1/2	1	1/2

Possible Descriptions: Athar Kurd pentachord on bottom; Hijaz tetrachord on 5th.

Nakriz

CD Disk 1 Track 26

C	D	Eb	F#	G	A	Bb	C
Do	Re	Mi bemol	Fa diaz	Sol	La	Si bemol	Do
1	1/2		1 1/2	1/2	1	1/2	1

Possible Descriptions: Nakriz pentachord on bottom; Hijaz tetrachord on 2nd; Nahawand tetrachord on 5nd.
Common in central mountain Greek tsamika-style dance music with clarinet lead. 2nd (Re) is heard as sub-dominant. It is frequently used in melodies as if it were the tonic. This turns out to be temporary as the tune finally resolves back to the 1st (Do).
In Arabic music, where Nakriz is very commonly used, it can also be called Zawil or Basandida when it is used as an ornamental modulation in Rast.

Bb-Based Maqams
Ajam Family

Associated Moods: Bright, happy, majesty, pride, loftiness, national anthems, strength, seriousness.

Ajam Ushayran (Bb Major)   *CD Disk 1 Track 27*

Bb	C	D	Eb	F	G	A	Bb
Si bemol	Do	Re	Mi bemol	Fa	Sol	La	Si bemol
1	1	1/2	1	1	1	1/2	

Possible Descriptions: Ajam or "Jaharka" pentachord on bottom; Ajam or "Jaharka" tetrachord on 5th; Farahfaza maqam on 6th; Ajam Ushayran is "relative major" to Farahfaza (G minor scale). Some say that the 3rd note in Ajam should be slightly flatter than the 3rd in a Western major scale. It is common to show a brief interlude into Ajam during taqasims based in Saba or Bayyati. This is accomplished by first emphasizing the 6th note in one of those maqams which is, of course, Bb. When Ajam is played on lower octaves it can be called Ajam Ushayran.

Shawq Afza

CD Disk 1 Track 28

Bb	C	D	Eb	F	Gb	A	Bb
Si bemol	Do	Re	Mi bemol	Fa	Sol bemol	La	Si bemol
1	1	1/2	1	1/2	1 1/2	1/2	

Possible Descriptions: Ajam or "Jaharka" pentachord on bottom; Hijaz tetrachord on 5th.

E half-flat-Based Maqams
Sikah Family

Associated Moods: Sacred, mystical. Common in folk melodies.

Huzam
CD Disk 1 Track 29

E half-flat		F	G	Ab		B	C	D	E half-flat
Mi nuss-bemol		Fa	Sol	La bemol		Si	Do	Re	Mi nuss-bemol
3/4		1	1/2	1 1/2		1/2	1	3/4	

Possible Descriptions: Sikah trichord on bottom; Hijaz pentachord on 3rd; Suznak maqam on 6th. The E half-flat in Huzam, Sikah and Mustaar (like Rast) is very slightly sharper than the E half-flat in Bayyati.

The notes in Huzam are the same as the notes in Suznak, but the tonic is on E half-flat instead of on C.

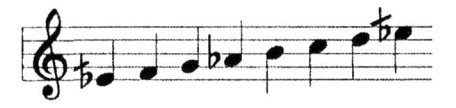

Sikah

CD Disk 1 Track 30

E half-flat	F	G	A	B half-flat	C	D	E half-flat
Mi nuss-bemol	Fa	Sol	La	Si nuss-bemol	Do	Re	Mi nuss-bemol
3/4	1	1	3/4	3/4	1	3/4	

Possible Descriptions: Sikah trichord on bottom; Rast pentachord on 3rd; Sikah trichord on 5th; Rast maqam on 6th.

The notes in Sikah are the same as the notes in Rast, but the tonic is on E half-flat instead of on C.

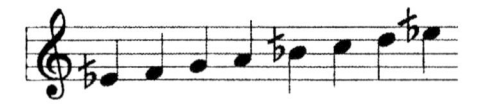

Mustaar

CD Disk 1 Track 31

E half-flat	F#	G	A	Bb	C	D	E half-flat
Mi nuss-bemol	Fa diaz	Sol	La	Si bemol	Do	Re	Mi nuss-bemol
1 1/4	1/2	1	1/2	1	1	3/4	

Possible Descriptions: Mustaar trichord on bottom; Nahawand pentachord on 3rd; Rast trichord on 6th.

Transposed D--Based Maqamat

Hijaz Kar (Shehnaz on C) — *CD Disk 2 Track 1*

C	Db	E	F	G	Ab	B	C
Do	Re bemol	Mi	Fa	Sol	La bemol	Si	Do
1/2	1 1/2	1/2	1	1/2	1 1/2	1/2	

Possible Descriptions: Hijaz pentachord on bottom; Hijaz tetrachord on 5th; Nakriz pentachord on the 4th.

Zanjaran (Shehnaz on C with Ajam)   *CD Disk 2 Track 2*

C	Db	E	F	G	A	Bb	C
Do	Re bemol	Mi	Fa	Sol	La	Si bemol	Do
1/2	1 1/2	1/2	1	1	1/2	1	

Possible Descriptions: Hijaz pentachord on bottom; Ajam pentachord on 4th.
Also called Zingaran or Zankulah.

Shad Araban (Shehnaz on G)   *CD Disk 2 Track 3*

G	Ab	B	C	D	Eb	F#	G
Sol	La bemol	Si	Do	Re	Mi bemol	Fa diaz	Sol
1/2	1 1/2	1/2	1	1/2	1 1/2	1/2	

Possible Descriptions: Hijaz pentachord on bottom; Hijaz tetrachord on 5th; Nakriz pentachord on the 4th.

Suzdil (Shehnaz on A)   *CD Disk 2 Track 4*

A	Bb	C#	D	E	F	G#	A
La	Si bemol	Do diaz	Re	Mi	Fa	Sol diaz	La
1/2	1 1/2	1/2	1	1/2	1 1/2	1/2	

Possible Descriptions: Hijaz pentachord on bottom; Hijaz tetrachord on 5th; Nakriz pentachord on the 4th.

Jaharka Turki (Shehnaz on F)   *CD Disk 2 Track 5*

F	Gb	A	Bb	C	Db	E	F
Fa	Sol bemol	La	Si bemol	Do	Re bemol	Mi	Fa
1/2	1 1/2	1/2	1	1/2	1 1/2	1/2	

Possible Descriptions: Hijaz pentachord on bottom; Hijaz tetrachord on 5th; Nakriz pentachord on the 4th.

Hijaz Kar Kurd (Kurd on C)

CD Disk 2 Track 6

C	Db	Eb	F	G	Ab	Bb	C
Do	Re bemol	Mi bemol	Fa	Sol	La bemol	Si bemol	Do
1/2	1	1	1	1/2	1	1	

Possible Descriptions: Kurd tetrachord on bottom; Kurd tetrachord on 5th.
Associated Moods: Lightly romantic.

Transposed C--Based Maqamat

Farahfaza (Nahawand on G)   *CD Disk 2 Track 7*

G	A	Bb	C	D	Eb	F	or	F#	G
Sol	La	Si bemol	Do	Re	Mi bemol	Fa	or	Fa diaz	Sol
1	1/2	1	1	1/2	1 or 1 1/2			1 or 1/2	

Possible Descriptions: Nahawand tetrachord on bottom; Hijaz tetrachord on 5th; or Nahawand tetrachord on bottom; Nahawand pentachord on 4th.
Associated Moods: Same as Nahawand.

Busalik (Nahawand on E)   *CD Disk 2 Track 8*

E	F#	G	A	B	C	D or D#	E
Mi	Fa diaz	Sol	La	Si	Do	Re or Re diaz	Mi
1	1/2	1	1	1/2	1 or 1 1/2	1 or 1/2	

Possible Descriptions: Nahawand tetrachord on bottom; Hijaz tetrachord on 5th; or Nahawand tetrachord on bottom; Nahawand pentachord on 4th. Some say that the third note in Busalik is slightly flatter than the Nahawand 3rd.

Yaka (Rast on G) (Rast Nawa)   *CD Disk 2 Track 9*

G	A	B half-flat	C	D	E	F half-sharp	G
Sol	La	Si nuss-bemol	Do	Re	Mi	Fa nuss-diaz	Sol
1	3/4	3/4	1	1	3/4	3/4	

Possible Descriptions: Rast pentachord on bottom; Rast tetrachord on 5th; Bayyati tetrachord on the 2nd; Husayni maqam on the 2nd; Bayyati trichord on the 6th.
Associated Moods: Same as Rast.

Hisar (Nawa Athar on D)

CD Disk 2 Track 10

D	E	F	G#	A	Bb	C#	D
Re	Mi	Fa	Sol diaz	La	Si bemol	Do diaz	Re
1	1/2	1 1/2	1/2	1/2	1 1/2	1/2	

Possible Descriptions: Nakriz pentachord on bottom; Hijaz tetrachord on 2nd; Hijaz tetrachord on the 5th.

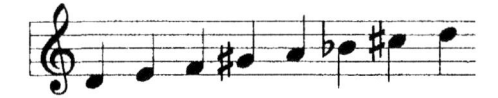

Transposed Bb--Based Maqamat

Jaharkah (Ajam on F) (F major) — CD Disk 2 Track 11

F	G	A	Bb	C	D	E	F
Fa	Sol	La	Si bemol	Do	Re	Mi	Fa
1	1	1/2	1	1	1	1/2	

Possible Descriptions: Ajam or "Jaharka" pentachord on bottom; Ajam or "Jaharka" tetrachord on 5th; Nahawand maqam on 6th; Jaharka is "relative major" to the Nahawand on D (D minor scale). Another definition of maqam Jaharka would replace the E with an E half-flat. And some say that the 3rd note in Jaharkah is slightly flatter than the 3rd in Ajam.

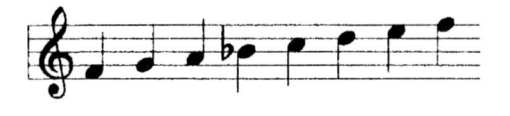

Transposed E half-flat--Based Maqamat

Rahat el Arwah (Huzam on B half-flat) *CD Disk 2 Track 12*

B half-flat	C	D	Eb	F#	G	A	B half-flat
Si nuss-bemol	Do	Re	Mi bemol	Fa diaz	Sol	La	Si nuss-bemol
3/4	1	1/2	1 1/2	1/2	1	3/4	

Possible Descriptions: Sikah trichord on bottom; Hijaz pentachord on 3rd; Suznak maqam on 6th.

Bastanikar (Huzam on B half-flat with Saba) *CD Disk 2 Trk 13*

B half-flat	C	D	E half-flat	F	Gb	A	B half-flat
Si nuss-bemol	Do	Re	Mi nuss-bemol	Fa	Sol bemol	La	Si nuss-bemol
3/4	1	3/4	3/4	1/2	1 1/2	3/4	

Possible Descriptions: Sikah trichord on bottom; Saba pentachord on 3rd.

Irak (Huzam on B half-flat with Bayati) *CD Disk 2 Track 14*

B half-flat	C	D	E half-flat	F	G	A	B half-flat
Si nuss-bemol	Do	Re	Mi nuss-bemol	Fa	Sol	La	Si nuss-bemol
3/4	1	3/4	3/4	1	1	3/4	

Possible Descriptions: Sikah trichord on bottom. Bayyati pentachord on 3rd.

Farahnak (Sikah on B half-flat)

CD Disk 2 Track 15

B half-flat	**C**	**D**	**E**	**F half-sharp**	**G**	**A**	**B half-flat**
Si nuss-bemol	Do	Re	Mi	Fa nuss-diaz	Sol	La	Si nuss-bemol
3/4	1	1	3/4	3/4	1	3/4	

Possible Descriptions: Sikah trichord on bottom. Rast pentachord on 3rd; Rast maqam on 6th.

40

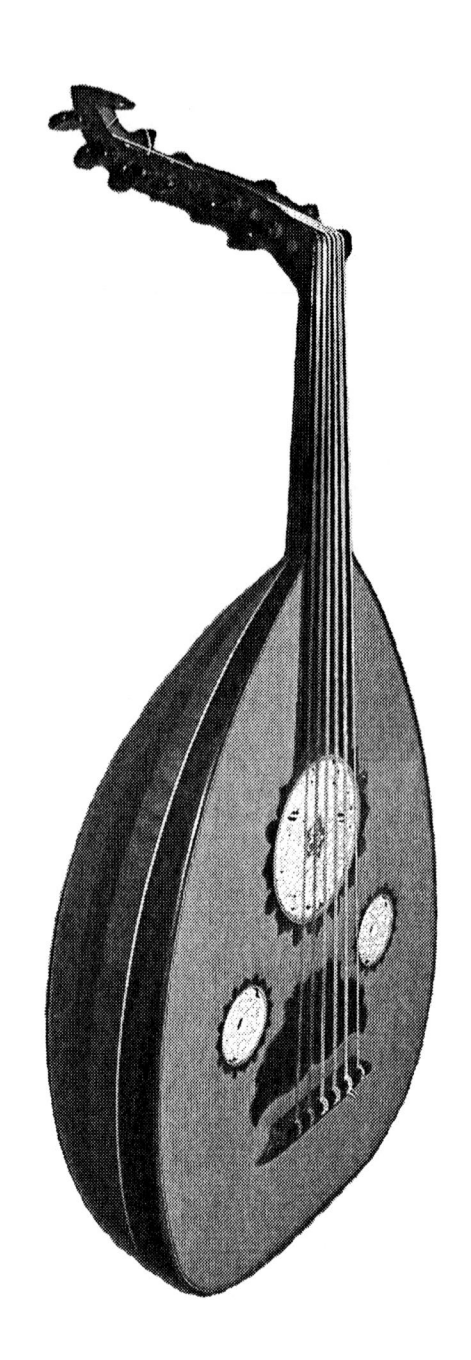

Modulations

Artfully and expressively moving from one maqam to another (yatahawwal in Arabic) is considered to be the supreme artistic achievement in sophisticated Middle Eastern music. This occurs both inside song structures and during improvisations (taqasim) which are a musician's opportunity to spontaneously compose.

Modulations within the D -- Based Maqamat

CD Disk 2 Track 16

Listen to Track 16 on CD2. You will hear improvised movements from Bayyati to Shuri (for just a brief moment) to Saba to Hijaz to Kurd... then back to Saba and, finally, Bayyati.

Some definitive maqam note changes:

Bayyati to Shuri: A becomes Ab and Bb becomes B natural (a Hijaz tetrachord replaces the Nahawand tetrachord in the upper part of the maqam.)

Bayyati to Saba: Gb appears above the F and the G natural vanishes.

Saba to Hijaz: Gb remains but the F vanishes and the E half-flat becomes Eb.

Hijaz to Kurd: Gb flattens to F

Kurd to Saba: Gb reappears and the F also remains. Eb becomes E half-flat. C may be used more clearly as a leading tone.

Saba to Bayyati: Gb vanishes and G natural reappears.

Modulations within the C -- Based Maqamat

CD Disk 2 Track 17

Listen to Track 17 on CD2. You will hear two parts.

1) You will hear improvised movements from Rast to Suznak to Nakriz (Zawil) (for just a moment)... then back to Rast.

Some definitive maqam note changes:

Rast to Suznak: A becomes G# and B half-flat becomes B natural (a Hijaz tetrachord replaces the Rast tetrachord in the upper part of the maqam.)

Suznak to Nakriz: E half-flat flattens to Eb and F sharpens to F#.

Nakriz to Rast: F# returns to F and Eb become E half-flat again.

2) You will hear improvised movements from Nahawand to Nawa Athar to Nakriz and then back to Nahawand.

Some definitive maqam note changes:

Nahawand to Nahawand: the upper tetrachord can appear as either Kurd or Hijaz with either the Bb or the B natural appearing.

Nahawand to Nawa Athar: F becomes F#.

Nawa Athar to Nakriz: the upper tetrachord changes from Hijaz to Nahawand -- the Ab becomes A natural and the B natural becomes Bb.

Nakriz to Nahawand: the upper tetrachord changes back to Kurd or Hijaz.

Transposing and Modulating between D and C Maqams
CD Disk 2 Track 18

As we pursue maqam studies we are frequently told that D and C -- Based Maqamat are seldom mixed together in the same song or improvisation. That is generally true if we leave the families in their home keys. But if we transpose either group to G, then the whole world of modulation possibilites from family to family opens up.

If we transpose the D-based families up a 4th (or down a 5th) to G or if we transpose the C-based families up a 5th (or down a 4th) to G all these movements between maqam families become possible!

Even within a single maqam, once we understand that the basic building blocks consist of "tetrachords", we see that this kind of transposition has already happened. "Tetrachords" can mean a series of 3 or 4 or 5 notes. Sometimes we say "trichords" or "pentachords" depending on how many notes we are describing, but these sequences of a few notes with certain intervals form the basic "building blocks" from which maqamat are constructed.

Consider, for example, the D-based maqamat: Hijaz, Bayyati and Kurd. Each of these maqams has a Nahawand "tetrachord" transposed up a 5th from C to G as its upper half.

Consider, for example, the D-based maqamat: Husayni and Hijaz Awji. Each of these maqams has a Rast "tetrachord" transposed up a 5th from C to G as its upper half.

Consider, for example, the C-based maqamat: Nahawand, Suznak and Nawa Athar. Each of these maqams has a Hijaz "tetrachord" transposed up a 4th from D to G as its upper half.

Practice these transposition and modulation exercises yourself:

1) Begin an improvisation in D-Based maqamat. Transpose the C-Based maqamat to G. When your improvisation leads you to G (the 4th above D), you then move through C-Based maqams in ways that appeal. Conclude your improvisation by returning through a D-Based maqam to end on D, the same place you began.

2) Begin an improvisation in C-Based maqamat. Transpose the D-Based maqamat to G. When your improvisation leads you to G (the 5th above C), you then move through D-Based maqams in ways that appeal. Conclude your improvisation by returning through a C-Based maqam to end on C, the same place you began.

D Maqams plus Rahat el Arwah   *CD Disk 2 Track 19*

Rahat el Arwah is Huzam transposed down a 4th from E half-flat to B half-flat. By making this transposition we create the possibility of moving from D-Based maqamat down a 1 3/4 step to B half-flat based maqams and then down another 1 3/4 step to Rast on G (Yakah).
Rahat el Arwah preserves the Hijaz "tetrachord", still beginning on D as part of its structure.
Bastanikar preserves the Saba "tetrachord", still beginning on D as part of its structure.
These are just a few of many examples of how maqams are built from tetrachord blocks.

Sample Modulations

CD Disk 2 Track 20

Listen to Track 20 on CD2 and try an discern the follow sequence of modulations. It is recorded twice: the second time with a voiceover explanation to help you follow.

Starting Point:	D Hijaz
Successive Modulations:	G Rast
	G Suznak
	G Nahawand
	D Hijaz
	B half-flat Rahat el Arwah
	G Suznak
	A Bayyati
	G Rast
Finishing Point:	D Hijaz.

Some definitive maqam note changes:

D Hijaz to G Rast: Bb becomes B half-flat

G Rast to G Suznak: the E becomes Eb and the F half-sharp becomes F#

G Suznak to G Nahawand: the B half-flat becomes Bb

G Nahawand to D Hijaz: the notes don't change but the movements serve to re-establish the tonic as D

D Hijaz to B half-flat Rahat el Arwah: decending sequence Eb, D, C to B half-flat moves the tonic down 1 3/4 steps

B half-flat Rahat el Arwah to G Suznak: the notes remain the same which the descending sequence B half-flat, A to G moves the tonic down another 1 3/4 steps

G Suznak to A Bayyati: the notes remain the same while a whole step up briefly places the tonic on A

A Bayyati to G Rast: the notes remain the same while a whole step back down returns the tonic to G and the upper notes are those of Rast on G (E and F half-sharp) instead of those of Suznak on G (Eb and F#)

G Rast to D Hijaz: B half-flat moves to Bb and then D is re-established as tonic

Table A: Note names of basic Arabic scale:

G:	Sol	Ramal Tuti or Jawab Nawa
F:	Fa	Mahuran
E half-flat:	Mi nuss-bemol	Buzrak
D:	Re	Muhayyar
C:	Do	Kirdan
B half-flat:	Si nuss-bemol	Awj
A:	La	Husayni
G:	Sol	Nawa
F:	Fa	Jaharka
E half-flat:	Mi nuss-bemol	Sikah
D:	Re	Dukah
C:	Do	Rast
B half-flat:	Si nuss-bemol	'Iraq
A:	La	Ushayran
G:	Sol	Yakah

Note: these names are of academic interest and are not commonly known by modern musicians.
These note names do not necessarily correlate with maqam names but it is possible to see obvious relationships.
Some of these words are originally Persian while others are Arabic. The presence of the Persian words doesn't mean that the scales used in contemporary Persian music are related to maqamat. Persian, Afghani, Pakistani and Hindu music scales have more similarity to each other than to the Arabic and Turkish scale system being taught in this book. It should also be noted that this book presents scales primarily from the Arabic way of teaching rather than the Turkish. But there is a great deal of overlap.

Table B: Note names of expanded basic Arabic scale:

G:	Sol	Ramal Tuti or Jawab Nawa
--		
Gb/F#	Sol bemol/Fa diaz	Jawab Hijaz
--		
F:	Fa	Mahuran
--		
E:	Mi	Jawab Busalik
E half-flat:	Mi nuss-bemol	Buzrak
Eb	Mi bemol	Sinbulah
--		
D:	Re	Muhayyar
--		
Db/C#	Re bemol/ Do diaz	Shahnaz
--		
C:	Do	Kirdan
--		
B	Si	Mahur
B half-flat	Si nuss-bemol	Awj
Bb	Si bemol	Ajam
--		
A:	La	Husayni
--		
Ab/G#	La bemol/Sol diaz	Hisar
--		
G:	Sol	Nawa
--		
Gb/F#	Sol bemol/Fa diaz	Hijaz
--		
F:	Fa	Jaharka
--		
E	Mi	Busalik
E half-flat:	Mi nuss-bemol	Sikah
Eb/D#	Mi bemol/Re Diaz	
--		
D:	Re	Dukah
--		
Db/C#	Re bemol/ Do diaz	Zirkulah
--		
C:	Do	Rast
--		
B	Si	Kawasht
B half-flat:	Si nuss-bemol	'Iraq
Bb	Si bemol	Ajam Ushayran
--		
A:	La	Ushayran
--		
Ab/G#	La bemol/Sol diaz	Qarar Hisar
--		
G:	Sol	Yakah

Note: the double hyphen "--" indicates the presence of another possible quartertone pitch for which the words "nim" (lower) and "tik" (higher) would be used before the nearest note name to provide a label.

Pitch Control on Traditional Arab-world Instruments

Fretless Stringed Instruments:

Plucked: Oud
Bowed: Rebab, Kemench, Violin, Cello, Bass

Fretless stringed intstruments yield all possible pitches depending on finger positioning. All maqamat can be easily played.

Fretted Stringed Instruments:

Plucked: Arabic Buzuk, Turkish Saz, Baglama, Tamboura
Bowed: Turkish Yayli Tambour

Fretted stringed instruments yield specific "quartertone" pitches. They commonly have 18 frets per octave instead of the 12 commonly found on well-tempered instruments. The common notes such as E half-flat, B half-flat, F half-sharp and A half-flat become available but other quartertones remain unplayable. It is only possible to play these instruments in certain pre-defined keys.

Wind Instruments:

Flutes: Arabic Nay, Turkish Ney
Reed: Arabic Mizmar, Mijwiz, Narghoul, Turkish Zurna, Clarinet, Accordion

The holes in these wind instruments are drilled to yield specific "quartertone" pitches. The common notes such as E half-flat and B half-flat become available but other quartertones and many halftones including E natural and B natural can only be played by "half-holing" (partially covering an open hole with part of a finger.) There is also considerable bending of note pitches possible through the use of mouth technique alone (embouchure.) Since it is difficult to play these instruments outside of certain pre-defined keys, instruments of different lengths are available.
The Clarinet is used in Turkey and pitch control is accomplished through mouth technique alone (embouchure.)
Accordions are a recent import into the Arab world and extra banks of reeds are added with common notes such as E half-flat and B half-flat included.

Zithers:

Plucked Zithers: Arabic Qanun, Turkish Kanun

The strings on these instruments have 5 to 9 moveable bridges, or mandrels, under them. By flipping these up and down, quartertone (or even finer) pitches can be set.

Hammered Zithers: Santur

Not common in Arabic or Turkish music except in Iraq. Common notes such as E half-flat and B half-flat are available on these instruments and they are used in maqam music.

Pitch Control on Other Instruments:

Keyboards:

Accoustic Pianos

It is not possible to play maqamat which include "quartertones."

Electronic Keyboards

Notes such as E half-flat, B half-flat, A half-flat, F half-sharp can quite easily be programmed into these keyboards and many pre-programmed models are available so that all maqamat can be played.

Other Fretted Stringed Instruments:

Plucked: Guitars, Banjoes, Bouzoukia, Mandolins, Balalaikas, etc

With 12 frets per octave, positioned for well-tempered intervals, it is not possible to play maqamat which include "quartertones."

Other Wind Instruments:

Flutes and Oboes: Open-Holed

If the holes are drilled for well-tempered intervals it is necessary to use combinations of "half-holing" (partially covering an open hole with part of a finger) and embouchure (mouth positions) in order to achieve quartertone pitches.

Flutes and Oboes: Keyed

It is very difficult to achieve quartertone pitches on these instruments unless it is a reed instrument which can easily yield mouth and breath controlled pitch bends.

Glossary of Terms:

Ajna
    Arabic word meaning "basic maqam building block" or sequence of notes. Translated as "tetrachord" or "trichord" or "pentachord."

Amal
    Arabic word meaning "the work." The creative process brought by a musician to building a musical improvisation.

Bemol
    French word imported into modern Arabic: "flat."

Diaz
    French word imported into modern Arabic: "sharp."

Dulab
    An introductory musical melody which is specific to a particular maqam.

Ghammaz
    Arabic word meaning "the wink of an eye." This term is used to label delicate musical decorations.

Half-flat
    A note played halfway between the pitch of the "natural," above, and the "flat," below.

Half-sharp
    A note played halfway between the pitch of the "sharp," above, and the "natural," below.

Interval
    Musicians frequently talk about intervals such as "5ths," meaning the 5th note in the scale. More strictly speaking, "harmonic intervals" are based on dividing musical intervals such as a whole octave into equal parts. A "harmonic 5th," for example, results from just such a division. However, since specific notes in a scale don't always fall on pitches defined by strict harmonic theory, the student should be aware that terms like the "2nd," "3rd," "4th," etc, can simply refer to the number of a note in a particular scale. When intervals are used to describe pitch differences less than a whole step, terms such as "half-step," "three-quarter-step," "quarter-step" or "quarter-tone" arise.

Koma
    An interval defined in Pythagorian musical theory but commonly used in Turkish maqam teaching literature to mean an increment of pitch equal to one-ninth of a whole step. Very precise pitch descriptions can be made using this term.

Maqam
: An Arabic or Turkish musical scale or mode. In older traditions, learning to perform and improvise in a particular maqam meant learning a whole world of standardized embellishments and phrases, beginnings and endings which are specific to a given maqam. Given the depth of each maqam, very few artists could manage to master more than a few in one lifetime. Specific emotions are typically associated with each maqam. English plural: "maqams." Arabic plural: "maqamat." Turkish spelling: "makam."

Modulate
: To change from on maqam to another. Sometimes the tonic, or "home base" note, remains the same during modulations and sometimes it changes.

Nuss Bemol
: Half flat.

Nuss Diaz
: Half sharp.

Penta-chord
: A sequence of 5 notes which form a building block in a maqam.

Qafla
: A traditional ending musical flourish for a particular maqam.

Quartertone
: Pitches approximately halfway between the well-tempered notes. Well tempered notes are all defined by either "whole-step" or "half-step" intervals. "Three-quarter-step" intervals create what we are calling "quartertones."

Reboton
: Half flat.

Shakhsiyyah
: A traditional opening musical flourish for a particular maqam.

Sikah
: Half flat. This term, although becoming common, is based on the Arabic note name for E half-flat. It is now becoming common to use it to refer to any half-flat. "Si sikah," for example, can refer to "B half-flat."

Solfege
: European syllables, Do Re Mi Fa Sol La Si, used to name notes in a scale. Unlike note names A B C D E F G, Do is portable and can be assigned to be the tonic of a scale at any absolute pitch. The note names in Indian music, Sa Re Ga Ma Pa Da Ni are roughly equivalent to Solfege syllables.

Taqasim
  Improvisation performed in Arabic music. Turkish spelling: "taksim" or "taxim."

Tetra-chord
  A sequence of 4 notes which form a building block in a maqam. The term "tetra-chord" is used generically to refer to any sequence of 3, 4 or 5 notes.

Tonic
  The "home base" note of a maqam or scale.

Transpose
  To move the "tonic" of a scale from one pitch to another. This can be done to accomodate the range of a singer's voice, in which case the whole framework of maqamat becomes portable. Or it can be done by designating a new "tonic" for a particular maqam so that it can interplay with other maqamat in pleasing ways.

Tri-chord
  A sequence of 3 notes which form a building block in a maqam.

Well-Tempered
  The scale which has become familiar in Europe and the Western world: 12 notes separated by "half-steps" which make up an octave.

Zaghrafa
  Musical ornamentations or decorations.

Acknowledgements:

I would like to acknowledge the many teachers who have helped me with maqam study. They include Haig Manoukian, George Lammam, Faruk Tekbilek, Simon Shaheen, Jihad Racy, Nabil Azzam, Joe Zeytoonian as well as many others who have taken the time to hang out with me in the music stores, music schools and personal homes in Cairo, Aleppo, Amman and many other places in the Arab world. Kadri Srour and Atef Abd el-Hameed are among these. Very special acknowledgement must go to Scott Marcus. His doctoral dissertation, "Arab Music Theory in the Modern Period" is a treasure of detailed information and this edition is largely based on categories of maqams which he created. The Arabic note name tables are also from his work. I would also like to thank the other members of Sherefé & The Habibis, my band, for all the time spent mutually approaching the infinitely fascinating world of maqams.

I would like to invite my teachers, as well as other teachers and students, to make corrections and additions to this introductory work. Hopefully, future editions will contain additional and more refined information.

I would also like to acknowledge that, since I am not a native Arab-world musician, that my recorded samples of various maqamat taqasims (improvisations) are to be taken as only a bare minimal introduction. The student will do well to find examples of taqasims played by Arab-world masters to listen to and to emulate. Maqamat are not only sequences of notes but also whole worlds of traditional stylized musical phrases with specific ornamentation specific to the instrument upon which they are played. I only hope that this book with these accompanying recordings can help the beginner establish a basic structure of knowledge of maqamat.

I would also like to mention that maqamat vary from region to region. It has been said that there are well over a hundred of them. The ones in this book are reflective of what is popular in Egypt, Jordan, Palestine, Syria and Lebanon. I have not attempted to focus, for example, on maqamat which are primarily known in Iraq. And I have not attempted to focus on Turkish makams, although there is considerable overlap.

Cameron Powers
cameron@rmi.net
303-449-4196

Cameron Powers -- Biography

Fascination with Peruvian Indian peoples encountered on mountaineering expeditions led Cameron to spend 8 years going to and from Andean villages back in the 1960's and 70's. He immediately discovered the value of learning to play their music with them as an easy aid to bonding in trust and friendship.
Cameron graduated with BA in Anthropology and Linguistics, University of Colorado, Boulder, with an emphasis on the study of Quechua, the language of the Incas.
Cameron also received a fellowship to attend a two-month intensive immersion program in Quechua at Cornell University. It was there that he began to realize the value of being a musician as well as a linguist.
Cameron also received a scholarship to work on a Doctoral program in Linguistics at the University of California, Berkeley. He continued to study the Inca language and began studies of the Tibetan language.
In 1973 Cameron lived in Greece with the Papanastassiou family and studied Greek language and Greek music.
Returning to Boulder, Colorado, Cameron performed Greek music and began the study of Arabic music with various local bands: "The Silk Route," "The Boulder Bouzouki Band," "Solspice," and "Sherefe."
He created Musical Instruments, built Houses, and helped produce a Spanish Language Teaching Program in Boulder while raising his children.
Cameron has a long association with Middle Eastern Music Camp which takes place every summer in Mendocino, California. He has studied with Nasser Musa, George Lammam, Haig Manoukian, Faruk Tekbilek, Nabil Azzam, and many others. He has studied with Simon Shaheen at Arabic Music Retreat in Mt. Holyoke, Mass. And he has studied with numerous musicians whom he has met on travels in the Middle East.
After the events in New York on 9/11, a pall was cast on his role as an American musician playing Middle Eastern Music. "Terrorism" had somehow entered the music. Gigs were cancelled; people became nervous about producing Middle Eastern Music-oriented shows.
Knowing full well from his travels in the Middle East and from his extensive chain of friendships with Middle Eastern musicians that there is a warm reception available to anyone, including Americans, who wish to travel the Middle East, he realized the importance of continuing his "musical missions."
Now back from Iraq, Egypt, Jordan, Lebanon, Syria and Palestine, he is working to help people understand the Arab psyche.

Other Books by Cameron Powers:

Singing in Baghdad

The story of events leading up to and including a journey to Baghdad, Iraq made at the same time as the US Marines were entering the city in the spring of 2003. The success of this journey illustrates the capacity of the Iraqi people to distinguish love-based invasions from fear-based invasions. The story told in Singing in Baghdad illustrates the possibility of expanding cross-cultural musical study and performance into a new kind of people-to-people international diplomacy.

Spiritual Traveler: Journeys Beyond Fear

Musicians have long held many of the keys to cross-cultural journeying as a spiritual path. Along the way many things are learned. In this book we find many clues about Arab-world people and the beauties of their ancient ways. With fear removed from our perceptions, we find a way paved for endless cross-cultural love affairs.

Additional copies of Arabic Musical Scales
or the books listed above can be ordered at:

Web: http://www.gldesignpub.com
or E-Mail: distrib@gldesignpub.com
or write to:
GL Design
2090 Grape Ave
Boulder, CO 80304   USA